Name a soup eaten by racists.

Klan Chowder.

♦

What's the definition of macho?

Running home from your own vasectomy.

♦

What do Robin Hood, a tiny prostitute, and a midget have in common?

They all have little johns.

♦

How can you tell an efficient nurse?

She can make a patient without disturbing the bed.

Books by Maude Thickett

Outrageously Offensive Jokes I
Outrageously Offensive Jokes II
Outrageously Offensive Jokes III

Published by POCKET BOOKS

Outrageously
OFFENSIVE JOKES III

MAUDE THICKETT

PUBLISHED BY POCKET BOOKS NEW YORK

This joke book may offend. That's why we called it *Outrageously Offensive Jokes*. The jokes included in this work are products of the author's imagination and fancy. No statements made about any person, product or place in any of these jokes should be taken as true.

Another *Original* publication of POCKET BOOKS

POCKET BOOKS, a division of Simon & Schuster, Inc.
1230 Avenue of the Americas, New York, N.Y. 10020

ISBN: 0-671-62884-4

First Pocket Books printing September, 1986

10 9 8 7 6 5 4 3 2 1

POCKET and colophon are registered trademarks
of Simon & Schuster, Inc.

Printed in the U.S.A.

For Stuart J. Miller, the man who made all this possible. A man of vision, a man with balls. May he attain his lifelong ambition of retiring to the Cape, where he will live out his days eating bearded clams.

Special thanks to Vinny V. for encouraging me to do this third book, and to Mr. Best for his wit and wisdom. Thanks, too, to all my wonderful friends at Pocket Sales, my immediate coworkers, the gang at "the show," my editor, and my friends throughout the country.

Contents

Outrageously
OFFENSIVE
JOKES
III

Hey, Leroy!

What are the words suburbanites fear most?

"Hi, we be yo' new neighbors."

◆

What do you say to a black woman who is begging you for sex?

How much?

◆

If a black man and an Irish woman were to have a baby, what would they call it?

A lepra-coon.

◆

How do black babies begin their lives?

As M&Mbryos.

◆

Why do black babies have such big heads?

So they don't fall out during the bridal dance.

◆

What do a lightly cooked steak and a black scholar have in common?

They're both considered rare.

◆

Name a soup eaten by racists.

Klan Chowder.

◆

What's black, has 32,000 legs, and has an IQ of 146?

Grambling College.

◆

In the black version of *Star Trek*, who was the first mate to Captain Kirk?

Mr. Spook.

◆

Define redundant.

A negro with a black eye.

What does PONTIAC stand for?

Poor Old Nigger Thinks It's A Cadillac.

Leroy and Jackson are standing at a bus stop. Leroy has a gash over his left eye.

"What happened, Leroy?"

"I was in church when fat ol' Lucy Evans sits down in front of me. When she gets up, her dress is tucked up in the crack of her ass. So being a gentleman, I pulls it out for her and BAM, the next thing I know, she hauls off and puts one upside my head."

The next week, Jackson sees Leroy again. This time he has a gash over his right eye.

"What happened to you?"

"Well, I was at church again and fat ol' Lucy Evans sits down in the pew right in front of me like before. She gets up and I see her dress is hanging down nice and smooth. I figure she likes it the way it was the last time, so I starts tucking it back in."

Why do you avoid hitting a black kid on a

ten-speed bike who is darting in and out of traffic?

Because it could be your bike.

◆

What do you call a black hitchhiker?

Stranded.

◆

How do they circumcise black babies in the Harlem hospital?

With a jigsaw.

◆

What do you call a high-rise in Harlem?

A Coon-dominium.

◆

What was little Thelma's favorite Christmas present last year?

A Cotton Patch Doll.

◆

What do you get when you cross a black and a WASP?

An abortion.

◆

What's the definition of a black family in Harlem?

A group of Negroes with keys to the same abandoned building.

◆

When a white baby dies, he goes to heaven, gets white wings, and is called an angel. What are black babies called after they get their black wings?

Bats.

◆

Why can't Stevie Wonder and Ray Charles read music?

Because they're black.

◆

Did you hear about the new maternity shop in Harlem?

It's called Mother Frockers.

◆

What do you call an orgy at an NAACP meeting?

Getting blackballed.

◆

What is a Hula-Hoop?

A teething ring for blacks.

◆

A huge, muscle-bound black man walks into a bar in an all-white neighborhood and asks the bartender for a drink. Taking a sip, he turns to the white man at his right and says, "I'm blacker than hell and I got a pecker named Mel and I just love fucking white women." The white man looks at the black guy, then sprints for the door.

The black man then turns to his left and says to the man sitting there, "I'm blacker than hell and I got a pecker named Mel and I just love fucking white women." The white guy says nothing, but immediately gets up and takes his drink to a far-off corner of the bar.

Then, totally enjoying himself, the black man bears down on a drunk little Polack and says with an evil grin, "I'm blacker than hell and I got a pecker named Mel and I just love fucking white women."

The Pole looks up at the huge black man and says in a drunken slur, "Listen, Mel, I don't blame ya. I wouldn't fuck a nigger either."

◆

What do you call one white guy with one black guy?

Liberal.

◆

What do you call one white guy with three black guys?

Victim.

◆

What do you call one white guy with five black guys?

Coach.

◆

What do you call one white guy with ten black guys?

Quarterback.

◆

What do you call one white guy with fifty black guys?

Boss.

◆

What do you call one white guy with one thousand black guys?

Warden.

◆

What do you call one white guy with twenty thousand black guys?

Postmaster General.

◆

What do you call one white guy with twenty million black guys?

Prime Minister of Rhodesia.

◆

One Sunday morning, a young black woman who needed forgiveness for her sins came to a Baptist church. She got up in front of the congregation and stated, "Last week, I slept with a young soldier who picked me up at a bar and I now ask the Lord's forgiveness."

"Hallelujah!" cried the congregation.

She continued, "Two days ago, I slept with a young sailor, but now I ask God's forgiveness."

"Hallelujah!" cried the congregation again.

"But tonight, because I have come here and done my penance, I will sleep with the Lord," she finished.

But before the congregation could respond, an old drunk in the back yelled out in a clear voice, "That's right momma, fuck 'em all."

◆

Why do blacks always have their hands down their pants?

Because Whitey took everything from them, but he ain't gonna get that.

◆

What do you get when you cross an alligator and a road runner?

A fifty-mile-an-hour nigger-chaser.

◆

What's the favorite game show in the South?

Maim that Coon.

Celebrities

Why didn't Dolly Parton ever take up stage acting?

They all said she'd be a big bust on Broadway.

♦

How do you know a man is really a bad dancer?

When he can still step on Dolly Parton's toes.

♦

What developed faster than a picture from a Polaroid One-Step?

Dolly Parton's breasts.

♦

What was Dolly Parton voted in high school?

Most likely to breast-feed Ethiopia.

♦

Why was Joan Collins voted most popular girl at the U.S. Cavalry dance?

Because she was mounted more times than the horses.

◆

What's the difference between the hosts of *Laugh-In* and propelling a boat while eating beans?

One is Rowan and Martin and the other is rowin' and fartin'.

◆

What would you call a Milky Way bar if it could walk and talk?

Gary Coleman.

◆

What did Sammy Davis, Jr.'s wife say to him before she went on vacation?

"Keep an eye on the house."

◆

What TV show did Sammy Davis, Jr. turn down a chance to appear on?

I Spy.

What is Sammy Davis, Jr.'s favorite cartoon character?

Popeye.

◆

Why is heaven losing money?

Because Rock Hudson is blowing all the prophets.

◆

Did you hear how popular Rock Hudson was?

He had neighbors up the ass.

◆

Did you know that Rock Hudson was going to make a movie with Sylvester Stallone?

They were going to call it *Ram-Butt*.

◆

Did you know that Rock Hudson had his auto insurance canceled three times?

He kept getting rear-ended.

◆

Did you hear that Jim Nabors died?

They found him bobbing up and down on the Hudson.

◆

Why did Rock Hudson's wife want a divorce?

Because he kept coming home shit-faced.

◆

What's a gay's greatest fantasy?

To be stuck between a Rock and a hard place.

◆

Did you hear that Rock Hudson was thinking about buying a cookie franchise?

He was going to call it Famous Anus.

◆

What did they find when they opened up Ronald Reagan's colon?

Rock Hudson's wristwatch.

◆

What did Rock Hudson, Henry the Eighth, and Donald Manes have in common?

They all fucked Queens.

◆

Why wasn't Donald Manes allowed on a golf course?

Because he slices when he drives.

◆

What did Donald Manes say when he was asked to assume the position of Queens Borough President?

"By God, I think I'll take a stab at it!"

◆

One thing you've got to say about Donald Manes . . .

He's a cut above the wrist.

◆

Did you hear about the new New York City Official Souvenir?

The Donald Manes Steak Knife Set.

◆

What was Donald Manes's favorite song?

"Mack the Knife."

◆

What were Donald Manes's last words on the night he was found by the police?

"See you later, dear, I'm going out for a couple of slices."

◆

Why would John F. Kennedy have made a bad boxer?

He couldn't take a shot to the head.

◆

What's pink and sticks out of a congressman's zipper?

Tip O'Neill.

◆

Why was Linda Ronstadt depressed?

Because she was down on the governor.

◆

What do you call a man accused of killing his wife at Christmas time?

Santa Claus Von Bulow.

◆

What did they call the Prince of Monaco when he went down on Princess Grace during her period?

Rudolph the Red-Nosed Rainier.

◆

What do you call Louis Farrakhan's arms and legs?

Mus-limbs.

◆

What do you call an Indian prime minister who dyes her hair?

Indira Blondie.

◆

What's seven feet tall, black, and makes up your hotel room?

Wilt Chambermaid.

◆

What is Charles Manson's favorite song?

"Call Me Irresponsible."

◆

What was Helen Keller's favorite song?

"Feelings (Nothing More Than Feelings)."

◆

What was Helen Keller's least favorite song?

"I Can See Clearly Now."

◆

What is the most useless thing for Helen Keller to own?

A mirror.

◆

How did Helen Keller lose her hand in the car?

By trying to read the stop sign.

◆

Why did Helen Keller get fucked on her first date?

She was never taught to say no.

◆

What do you call a midget with sores on his penis?

Herpes Villachaise.

◆

What do you call a gay German pianist?

Libernazi.

◆

What kind of coffee did Marie Antoinette drink?

Decapitated.

◆

What's the name of the bald actor who dices food?

Yul Blender.

◆

What's white and comes in Brownies?

Roman Polanski.

◆

What's black, weighs 350 lbs., and eats pancakes?

Uncle Jemima.

◆

Why did Captain Kirk piss on Lt. Uhura's neck?

He wanted to go where no man has gone before.

♦

What do Philadelphia hockey player Pelle Lindbergh and pilot Charles Lindbergh have in common?

They are both dead flyers.

♦

What do you call O.J. Simpson's jock?

An All-American ball carrier.

♦

Who's white, 60 years old, and caught his dick in a popcorn machine?

Orville Reddencocker.

♦

What kind of car does Renée Richards drive?

A convertible.

♦

Why is Billie Jean King such a good tennis player?

Because she swings both ways.

◆

Why does Santa Claus only have seven reindeer?

Because Prancer moved in with a hairdresser in Beverly Hills.

◆

Why did Frosty the Snowman pull down his pants?

He heard the snowblower coming.

◆

What do you call a famous black singing group with the clap?

Gladys Knight and the Drips.

◆

What sucks your blood while flipping pancakes?

Count Spatula.

◆

Why was Joan Collins voted "Woman of the Year" by *Screw* Magazine?

Because she had more meat between her buns than McDonald's.

◆

What cereal does Linda Lovelace eat for breakfast?

Kellogg's Porn Flakes.

◆

Have you heard about the new John Wayne toilet paper?

It's rough, it's tough, and it doesn't take shit off of nobody.

◆

What do you call a man on the Ponderosa dying of an infected wound?

Lorne Gangrene.

Iranians, Arabs, and Other Sand Fleas

What's worse than being hijacked by Iranians?

Being rescued by Egyptians.

◆

Did you hear about the one-legged Iranian woman who was raped?

She couldn't cross her legs to save her ass.

◆

What's a queer Arab?

One who speaks with tongue in sheik.

◆

What do you call a Libyan who cleans camel stalls for a living?

An executive.

◆

What do you get when you cross a potato and Muammar el-Qaddafi?

A dick tater.

◆

What is Muammar el-Qaddafi spelled backward?

Who cares—let's shoot the cocksucker!

◆

What do you call a soft, out of shape Libyan leader?

Mallowmar el-Qaddafi.

◆

What do the Ayatollah Khomeini's followers think of him?

They think he's hot Shiite.

◆

What do Arabs do on a Saturday night?

Sit under palm trees and eat their dates.

Why don't Iranians get hemorrhoids?

Because they are such perfect assholes.

◆

What happens to Egyptian girls who forget to take the pill?

They become mummies.

◆

Did you hear about the Iranian who had an asshole transplant?

The asshole rejected him.

◆

What do they use for underarm deodorant in Iran?

Raid.

◆

What's the definition of gross ignorance?

144 Iranians.

What do Iranian men use as cock rings?

Flea collars.

◆

Did you hear about the planeload of retarded Poles who emigrated to Iran?

They raised the average IQs of both countries.

◆

What do you get when you cross an Iranian with a monkey?

A retarded monkey.

◆

What do you have when you've got 50,000 Iranians at the bottom of the ocean?

A good start.

◆

If an Iranian and a Libyan jump out of an airplane without parachutes, which one would hit the ground first?

Who cares?

◆

Did you hear about the Iranian who came back disappointed from the car dealership?

He thought a vulva was a fancy car from Sweden.

◆

What's transparent and lives in the gutter?

A Libyan with the shit kicked out of him.

◆

In darkest Africa, two cannibals walk into a neighborhood restaurant and ask to see the menu. The waiter points to the blackboard, which lists the offerings of the day.

Poached Portuguese	$10.50
Fried American	$12.50
Sauteed Spaniard	$ 9.50
Stuffed Arab	$20.00

"Hey, how come the Arab is so much more expensive?" the first cannibal asks.

The waiter looks disgusted and says, "Man, you ever try cleaning one of those fuckers?"

◆

Why were rectal thermometers banned in Iran?

They caused too much brain damage.

◆

How do Libyan people make babies?

They wear each other's underwear.

◆

What do you get when you cross an Iranian with a pig?

Nothing. There are some things even a pig won't do.

◆

What's the difference between a Libyan and a bucket of shit?

The bucket.

What's Up, Doc?

What's the definition of a practical nurse?

A nurse who marries a wealthy old cancer patient.

♦

What's the definition of macho?

Running home from your own vasectomy.

♦

What's the difference between a bartender and a proctologist?

A proctologist deals with only one asshole at a time.

♦

What's the difference between an anthropologist and a gynecologist?

One looks up your family tree and the other looks up your family bush.

◆

How can you tell an efficient nurse?

She can make a patient without disturbing the bed.

◆

What do you call a prick with V.D., gonorrhea, AIDS, sores, and blisters?

A hot dog with the works!

◆

How did the leper fail his driving test?

He left his foot on the gas.

◆

How come the leper couldn't speak?

The cat got his tongue.

◆

How come nobody in the leper colony could walk after the war?

They were defeeted.

Three prospective mothers were sitting in the doctor's office waiting to see the doctor. The first one said, "When my husband and I were making love, I was underneath him. The doctor says I'll have a boy." The second woman said, "When my husband and I were making love, I was on top. The doctor said we'll have a girl." Suddenly, the third woman started to cry hysterically. "Oh shit. I'm going to have puppies!"

What disease can you get if you stick your dick in a dirty can of Coke?

Burpies.

What's the leading cause of death among Italian coal miners?

Black Lunguine.

Define Band/Aids.

A new disease affecting gay musicians.

♦

What's the difference between a proctologist and a grade one detective?

None. They're both crack investigators.

♦

A man walks into the doctor's office with a bright red ring around his penis. Frantically, he asks the doctor for help. The doctor studies the situation, then says, "I can fix this."
   "How much?" asks the man.
   "Twenty-five dollars," says the doctor.
   "But the last doctor said it was very expensive to treat."
   "Either the other doctor was blind or never saw lipstick before."

Goldstein, Goldman, and Goldberg

What kind of cigarettes do rabbis smoke?

Gefiltered.

◆

What do you get when you cross Arnold Schwarzenegger and a garment district Jew?

Conan the Wholesaler.

◆

What was the name of the first Jewish astronaut?

Nose Cohen.

◆

Define JAP nymphomaniac.

A Jewish woman who has to have it at least once a month.

◆

What do you get when you pick up a Jewish frog?

Shwarts.

♦

How do two Jews engage in oral sex?

They sit at opposite ends of the bedroom and yell "Fuck you."

♦

What do you call a tie-breaker in a Jewish beauty contest?

A "Fuck-off."

♦

What do you call twelve Jewish women in a swimming pool?

The bay of pigs.

♦

Did you hear about the Kosher-Mexican restaurant?

It's called the Casa Hadassah.

Have you heard about the new JAP horror movie?

Debbie Does Dishes.

◆

What was the name of the famous Jewish bank robber in the Old West?

Billy the Yid.

◆

What do you call bad Jewish deli meat?

Pusstrami.

◆

What is the number one dishwashing liquid in Israel?

Palmolive Goldberg.

◆

What do you call an Israeli air strike?

Blintzkrieg.

Two hookers were sunning themselves beside a pool at a Miami Beach hotel and comparing notes.

"I got $300 yesterday for doing it with this really old guy. I had to suck him off while his wife watched."

"Gross!" exclaimed the second whore.

"No, his name was Goldberg."

◆

Three men—an Italian, an Englishman, and a Jew—were captured by the Nazis. The German officer in command had them brought to his office, and told them he would only let them go if their penis sizes totaled one foot.

The Italian whipped out his penis and it measured seven inches. The Englishman's measured four and one-half inches. The Jew dropped his pants, and was measured at one-half inch. A sigh of relief was made by all three men.

As they left the Nazi camp, the Italian bragged, "If it wasn't for my seven inches, we'd still be prisoners."

The Englishman countered with, "Well, old man, if it wasn't for my four and a half, we'd have never gotten out."

The Jew then piped up and bragged, "If it

wasn't for my hard-on, we'd have been gon-ers."

◆

What's the Yiddish definition of a diaphragm?

A trampoline for schmucks.

◆

What is a bathroom menace?

A Jewish man circumcised by a cross-eyed rabbi.

◆

Did you hear about the new Jewish Cadillac?

It stops on a dime . . . then picks it up.

◆

What's the most popular game show in Israel?

The Price Is Right.

◆

How do you keep a JAP sexually stimulated during sex?

Stick a sale sign on the ceiling.

◆

What sucks but doesn't swallow?

A Jewish girl.

◆

What do you call 5,000 JAPS converging at Bloomingdales during a sale?

Yid-lock.

◆

What does a JAP call a French kiss?

Eating kosher tongue.

◆

What are a Jewish baby's first words?

Trust fund.

◆

What do you call a vicious Jew rampaging through Europe?

Genghis Cohen.

Various Villainies

Why don't unborn babies have to go out shopping for food?

They get womb service.

◆

What does a French cruise missile say?

Ooh la la BABOOM.

◆

What do a first mate on a ship and a date who licks your ass have in common?

They both swab the poop deck.

◆

What is the difference between a sloppy tie and a hunchback?

You could straighten the tie.

◆

What's the difference between a shot of Novocaine in the ass and a hobo's right ball?

One's a numb butt and the other's a bum nut.

◆

What do you call a weasel's vagina covered with ice cream?

Pie à la mole.

◆

What do you call a musical group that sings about prophylactics?

A rubber band.

◆

What do you call nerds at the Quaker Oats Company?

Checkerboard squares.

◆

What would you call a midget fortuneteller who escapes from jail?

A small medium at large.

◆

What do a farming family and a defecating man have in common?

They're all squatters.

♦

What do you call it when your head is caught up a gorilla's ass?

Stuck behind the ape ball.

♦

When do you know you're in a yuppie neighborhood?

When the fire department only uses Perrier water.

♦

What is the difference between a Southern treat and an ice cream used in sexual acts?

One is a corn pone and the other is a porn cone.

♦

What is the difference between a scar made by kissing and a famous baseball player's ass?

One is a hickey mole and the other is a Mickey hole.

◆

What's the difference between a comfortable foot covering and a defecating Indian?

One is a sitting shoe and the other is a shitting Sioux.

◆

What is the definition of endless love?

Two blind people playing tennis.

◆

When do you know it's too cold outside to go for a walk?

When your dog sticks to the fire hydrant.

◆

What do you call a mean dog taking a leak?

A Doberman pisser.

◆

Confucius says, "One must live by a dog's rule of life: if you can't eat it or fuck it, piss on it."

◆

What's it called when a bank guard takes a shit?

A security deposit.

◆

What do you call a bunch of people drooling in army uniforms?

The Salivation Army.

◆

What do you get when a drummer takes a bullet in the ass?

A rim shot.

◆

One nice summer day Papa Mole, Mama Mole, and Baby Mole were burrowing in the ground. Suddenly, Papa Mole starts to sniff the air inside the tunnel. "I smell whiskey," he says, and continues to burrow.

From behind, Mama Mole proclaims, "I

smell maple syrup." She too continues on her way.

Shortly after, Baby Mole also stops, takes a sniff, and says brazenly, "Funny, I smell molasses."

♦

What do you call 250 squaws without breasts?

The Indianippless 500.

♦

How do you know you're not going to have a good day?

When, in the morning, you open the refrigerator door and the rump roast farts in your face.

♦

Why do cannibals rejoice when a neighboring tribe's women are pregnant?

Because they know where their next meal is coming from.

Eye-talians, or Never Let a Dago By

What's the difference between Bigfoot and an Italian mother?

One is five foot ten, smells, and has matted hair all over its body. The other has big feet.

◆

Who really assassinated John F. Kennedy?

Two hundred Italian sharpshooters.

◆

Why do Italian organ grinders always have monkeys with them?

Somebody has to do the books.

◆

How did you know you were captured by the Italian Army during World War II?

When you looked out the window of your prison cell, you saw the firing squad in a circle.

Luigi turns eighteen on March 26. On March 27, his father takes him to the local whorehouse so Luigi can become a real man.

"Just tell the girl you want 69," said the father, trying to break his son in gently.

"Okay, Papa," says Luigi shyly.

The boy gets up to the room with the prostitute and tells her he wants to do 69. She takes off her clothes, and then removes his. As she is about to mount him, she farts. She gets up and opens the window, waves the odor out of the room, and then closes the window.

The whore comes back over to the bed and begins to mount the boy again. As she is about to lower her groin to his face, she farts again. She gets up, goes over to the window, opens it, and begins to wave the odor out again. She turns around and sees the boy getting dressed.

"Where are you going, sweetheart?" she asks. "I'll be right there."

Luigi looks her straight in the eye and says, "If you think I'm going to sit through 67 more of those, you're nuts."

◆

What do you call an obese Italian pool player?

Minestrone Fats.

◆

Did you hear about the new disease in Italy that affects male genitals?

It's called Bocci Balls.

◆

An Arab and an Italian tourist are traveling through the desert on camelback. In the middle of the tour, at the height of the heat, the camel starts to lose its energy, and the Arab realizes his mount needs water. They finally get to a water hole, but the camel refuses to drink. The Arab and the Italian wet his lips, but have no luck getting the camel to drink. They offer water to him in a bucket, but still no luck. Finally, the Arab gets an idea.

"Listen," says the Arab, "let's make out like he's a straw. I'll stick his head under the water and you suck on his asshole. The water has to get in him for sure."

"Great idea," says the Italian, and so they start. About fifteen minutes into the procedure, the Italian starts to gag.

"What's the problem?" asks the Arab.

"I think you've got his head down a little too deep. I seem to be bringing up a lot of mud from the bottom."

◆

Why wouldn't the Italian athlete drink anything after the track meet?

He was afraid he'd contract Gator-Aids.

◆

Why did the Italian buy twelve pairs of underwear?

He had to have one for each month.

◆

Why is Italian bread so long?

So they can dip it into the sewer.

◆

What's black, crisp, and sits on the roof?

An Italian electrician.

◆

Did you hear about the Italian girl who wanted to dress in style?

She knew lace stockings were in, so she wore black stockings and never shaved her legs.

Two Italian girls just off the boat were walking to the store when one said to the other, "Yesterday, I found a rubber on the patio."

Her friend replied, "What's a patio?"

◆

An Italian stud on the make sauntered up to a pretty coed on campus and said, "Hey, honey, why don't you come up to my place for a good time after school this afternoon?"

"No thanks," the girl replied, "I'm a lesbian."

At a loss for a way to keep the conversation going, the Italian stud said, "No kidding! So what do you think of the situation in Beirut?"

◆

What do you call a bunch of sightless Italians in Venice?

Venetian Blinds.

◆

Did you hear about the Italian prizefighter who had a Roman nose?

It was roamin' all over his face.

◆

What do you call an Italian explorer who tells fortunes?

Crystal Ball Columbus.

◆

What do you get when you cross a lion with an Italian?

Something that doesn't make any sense, but you listen to it anyway.

◆

What's the name of the Italian director who makes hack and slash movies?

Dino De Demented.

In a Word, Sex

What is the difference between a chicken caught in a wind machine and anal sex?

One is a cluck in the fan and the other is a fuck in the can.

♦

Did you hear that the Playboy channel and a children's channel are getting together on Cable TV?

They're going to call it Nipplelodion.

♦

What's the difference between a cook and a perverted aquarium owner?

One fixes dishes and the other dicks his fishes.

♦

Did you hear about the Hollywood actress who made it the hard way?

She had talent.

What do breasts and train sets have in common?

They're both for children, but daddies can't resist playing with them too.

◆

What is the difference between eleven men screwing one woman and a motorcycle mama?

One is a gang bang and the other bangs gangs.

◆

When can you be sure your girlfriend is a great cocksucker?

When you have to pull the sheets out of the crack in your ass.

◆

What fantastic advertising idea did the madam use to increase her business at the whorehouse?

Scratch and sniff business cards.

◆

George was sitting at a bar with his best friend Louie. As they sipped their drinks, George complained to Louie, "I don't know what to do. During sex, my wife never comes at the same time I do."

"Hey, man, that's no problem," says Louie. "Do what I do. Keep a small handgun under your pillow. Just when you get the urge to shoot your wad, fire a shot. It works like a charm. I should know—me and my wife had the same problem."

"Great, I think I'll try it tonight," George says. He pays his tab and hurries home.

That very night, Louie gets an urgent call from George's wife, telling him to run down to the local hospital; George was calling for him.

As Louie enters the room, he sees George lying in bed in obvious pain.

"What happened to you?"

"Shit, Louie, you wouldn't believe it. I did what you said with the gun, you know. Gracie says let's 69, so we 69. I'm just about to come, so I pull out the gun and shoot."

"And?" prompted Louie.

"And," George continues, "she bites the tip of my cock off and farts in my face!"

♦

What two things are great to ride until your friends see you on them?

Fat women and mopeds.

♦

What is the definition of coyote love?

It's waking up trapped in bed with a woman so ugly that, rather than risk arousing her by removing your arm from under her head, you bite it off at the shoulder.

♦

What do Johnson & Johnson and a walrus have in common?

They are both looking for a tighter seal.

♦

What do you throw at a wedding where the bride is pregnant?

Puffed Rice.

♦

Why don't debutantes like gang bangs?

Too many thank-you notes to write.

♦

Why do men wish women were more like hockey games?

Because hockey games only have 20-minute periods.

◆

What's the perfect gift for the man who has everything?

Penicillin.

◆

What's the difference between a dance for sailors and a mermaid?

One is a seamen's ball and the other balls seamen.

◆

Did you hear about the new commemorative stamp for prostitutes?

It costs twenty-two cents. Fifty if you want to lick it.

◆

What did the ex-prostitute get for a gift at her bridal shower?

His and Herpes towels.

◆

What is the difference between a young actress and a prostitute?

A prostitute doesn't drive a BMW.

◆

Do you know why a bald man always has a hole in his pocket?

So he can scratch his hair once in a while.

◆

What is the difference between a sin and a shame?

It's a fucking sin to stick it in and a fucking shame to pull it out.

◆

Did you hear the one about the unfortunate voyeur?

He was arrested at the peek of his career.

◆

At the funeral of her husband, the young widow was surrounded by her friends and relatives. To her sister, she sobbingly told of her love life.

"It was marvelous. He had such a wonderful, powerful stroke. He'd even keep time with the church bells on Sunday morning."

"I heard he died in bed of a heart attack. Is that true?" her sister pried.

"It sure is. In fact, if it wasn't for that damn fire house next door, he would still be here with us today."

◆

What do Robin Hood, a tiny prostitute, and a midget have in common?

They all have little johns.

◆

Two real estate agents are sitting at a booth in a diner. One of them says to the other, "Shit, business is down. If I don't sell more houses this year, I'm going to lose my fucking ass!"

Seeing a pretty young woman sitting in the next booth, he suddenly realizes how loud his voice had gotten.

"Sorry about the strong language," he apologizes sheepishly.

"Oh, that's okay," the girl says. "If I don't

sell more ass this year, I'm gonna lose my fuckin' house!"

◆

What is the best way to avoid rape?

Beat off your attacker.

◆

What's worse than finding lipstick on your husband's collar?

Finding nipple rouge behind his ears.

◆

Seven-year-old Bobby and six-year-old Nancy were listening through their big sister's keyhole while she was entertaining her boyfriend. After they'd heard much moaning and groaning, they heard their sister sigh, "Oh, Joe, you're in where no man has been before."

Bobby and Nancy turned to each other and said, "Wow, he must be fucking her in the ass."

◆

Two nine-year-old boys are in their back yards arguing back and forth over their fence.

"My dog is better than your dog."

"Is not!"

"My bike is better than yours."

"Is not!"

"My Mom is better than yours."

At this, the other boy stops and says, "Well, maybe. But only because I've heard my father say so too!"

◆

What is a double-bagger?

A woman so ugly that, before you'll fuck her, you put a bag over her head and one over yours—in case hers falls off.

◆

A man walks into a doctor's office and asks the doctor if it is possible for him to get a larger penis.

"Of course," says the doctor, "but you'll need a transplant."

"That sounds okay to me, Doc; let me see what you got."

So the doctor goes into the back and returns shortly with a six-inch penis.

"Hmmm," says the man, "you got anything larger?"

The doctor goes back into the storeroom and returns with a nine-inch penis.

"You know, Doc, if I'm gonna do this, I might as well do it right. Bring me the biggest one you got."

The doctor comes back with a twelve-inch cock this time, and lays it on his desk.

"That's perfect," says the patient, "but do you have one in white?"

Pea-Brained Poles

What did Jesus say to the Polish people as he was hanging on the cross?

"Play it dumb till I get back."

♦

Why did the Polish girl tattoo her zip code on her thighs?

So she could get male in her box.

♦

Why did the elderly Polish woman have her tubes tied?

She thought six grandchildren were enough.

♦

Why do Poles make the best astronauts?

Because they all take up space in school.

♦

What was the Polish Pope's first miracle?

He heeled a dog.

◆

Why didn't the Polish mother want her daughter to become an RN?

She heard they had nurse's AIDS.

◆

Why did the Pole plant Cheerios in his garden?

Because he thought they were bagel seeds.

◆

What's a $3.50 Polish cocktail?

A glass of water with a lime in it.

◆

Did you hear about the Pole named Joe Shits who wanted to change his name?

He did; to John.

Why did the Pole jerk off at thirty thousand feet?

He wanted to be a skyjacker.

◆

An enterprising young man gets a job in a sleazy porno shop in the red-light district. The manager leaves for lunch, putting the kid in charge of the store.

Soon, a white woman walks in and asks, "How much for that white dildo?"

"Ten dollars," replies the boy. She decides to take it, and he wraps it up for her.

Then a black woman walks in and asks, "How much for that black dildo?"

"Twenty dollars," says the boy, wrapping it up for her.

Then a Polish woman walks in and asks, "How much is that plaid dildo?"

"Fifty dollars," says the boy as he quickly wraps it up for her.

A little while later, the manager returns and asks how business was while he was out.

"Great," says the boy excitedly. "I sold a white woman a white dildo for ten dollars, then I sold a black woman a black dildo for twenty dollars, then a Polish woman came in and I sold her your thermos for fifty dollars!"

Did you hear about the newest invention from Poland?

It's a solar-powered flashlight.

◆

How did the Polish hemophiliac die?

He went to an acupuncturist.

◆

A Pole walked into a drugstore and asked the woman for some deodorant.

"The spray kind or the ball kind?"

Stopping to think for a minute, the Pole answered, "Give me the spray kind. I don't think my wife ever complained about my crotch smelling."

◆

What's a Polish ménage-à-trois?

Using both hands to masturbate.

◆

Why don't people in Warsaw enjoy spectator sports in the local arena?

Because everywhere you sit you're seated behind a Pole.

◆

The vice president of a midtown construction job came across an odd sight as he approached the Italian carpenters who worked for him. There, in the middle of an unfinished ceiling, was Guiseppe, hanging like a monkey.

"Hey, you dumb wop, what the fuck do you think you're doing?" screamed the V.P.

"I'm a chandelier," claimed Guiseppe.

"Get your ass down from there before I fire you," threatened the V.P.

After several warnings, the V.P. had no choice but to fire the Italian. Thinking he had rid himself of all his problems, the V.P. got an unpleasant surprise the next day when he found all his Polish laborers walking off the job. Finding the spokesman for the group, the V.P. demanded to know why they were leaving. With his head held out stubbornly, the Pole replied, "We ain't working without lights, and that's final."

Fruits and Nuts

What is a drag race in San Francisco?

Rush hour.

What's the difference between a vulture and a male hairdresser?

A vulture won't eat a man until after he's dead.

How did the two drunk gays at a bar settle their argument?

They went outside and exchanged blows.

Did you hear about the new Faggot Patch Doll?

It comes with AIDS and a death certificate.

What's in the air in Greenwich Village that keeps women from getting pregnant?

Men's legs.

◆

What's the name of the famous North American Man/Boy Love Association outlaw twosome?

Butch Cassidy and the No-Pants Kid.

◆

What do you call rubber sheets in a house full of gays?

Golden shower curtains.

◆

Why did the Italian lesbian cut her trip to America short?

She missed her native tongue.

◆

What position did the gay teacher seek when he joined the faculty of an all-boys school?

Headmaster.

◆

What do you call a bike rider who swings both ways?

A bi-cyclist.

◆

What did the gay Indian want more than anything else?

A few bucks to eat on.

◆

What do the Moral Majority and San Francisco gays have in common?

They both suck.

◆

What did the gay wolf do to the little pig?

He huffed and he puffed and he blew his drawers down.

◆

Did you hear about the gay college student who got a job in the circumcision room at the local hospital?

He only makes three dollars an hour, but the tips are great and there's a good chance to get a head.

◆

What's gay and comes in your washing machine?

The Mayfag repairman.

◆

How can a gay man protect himself from contracting the deadly AIDS virus?

Sit down and keep his mouth shut.

◆

How did the Statue of Liberty get AIDS?

From Staten Island fairies.

◆

Have you heard about the new AIDS clinic in Dallas?

It's in a skyscraper downtown called "Six Fags Over Texas."

◆

A man walked into a florist shop and asked if they wired flowers long distance. The proper-looking young woman behind the counter said yes.

"How about the West Coast?"

"No problem," she replied.

"I'll be back" he said, and he left.

The next day he returned, with a battered, bloodied, frail-looking man in tow. The shocked clerk asked, "What's the meaning of this?"

"This is my brother. Wire him to San Francisco. He's a fucking pansy."

◆

Two female executives on a business trip were sharing a hotel room together. The first night, after the lights were out, one woman came over to the other's bed and started to caress her shoulder.

"There's something I want to tell you, and I don't know how to say it, so I'll just be frank . . ."

Rising from her bed, the other one said, "No, I'll be Frank."

A Jewish gay and a Polish gay were sitting in a New York bar discussing their summer vacation plans.

"I'm going home to Poland," said the Polish gay, hoping to impress the Jew.

"Well," said the Jewish gay, "*I'm* looking for something really different this year. I think I'll go to one of the isolated Caribbean islands. But I can't decide if I should pay the extra bucks to fly directly to the island or just take the ferry."

"What fairy?" asked the Polish gay coyly.

"The ferry *boat*," replied the Jewish gay, exasperated.

"How delightful!" screamed the Polish gay. "I didn't know we had a navy!"

◆

Jesse James and his gang attacked a train just outside Dodge City. They went through each car and lined up all the travelers. Jesse entered, faced the people, and yelled, "All right, suckers, we're going to rape all the men and rob all the women."

His brother Frank turned to him and said, "Jesse, you mean we are going to rape all the women and rob all the men."

With that, a little faggot stood up, pointed his finger at Jesse, and yelled at Frank, "Hey, he's the boss."

◆

What's the definition of a bisexual?

Someone who likes girls as well as the next guy.

◆

What do you call five gay blacks butt-fucking?

A soul train.

◆

Why did the homosexual get beaten up in the bar?

He walked in, stuck out his tongue, and asked the bartender to put a head on it.

◆

What's the definition of optimism?

A ninety-year-old gay who still shaves his legs.

◆

Define latent homosexuality.

Swishful thinking.

Remember
the Alamo!

What was the name of the Mexican character who replaced Leonard Nimoy in *Star Trek*?

Mr. Spic.

◆

Why do Mexicans have such fat wallets?

They're full of food stamps.

◆

Did you hear about the famous Mexican trumpet player who opened up a whorehouse?

It's called Herb Alpert and the Tijuana Ass.

◆

What is a Mexican day in the country?

Chasing roaches in a vacant lot.

◆

What is the official Mexican mascot?

The litterbug.

◆

Why did little Juan win an award at the El Paso PTA banquet?

He always had the most parents at the meeting.

◆

Did you hear about the Mexican woman who had twins?

They named one José and the other Hose B.

◆

What's the first lesson you learn at a Mexican driving school?

How to open a locked car with a coat hanger.

◆

Why aren't there any vampires south of the border?

Every time they suck Mexican blood they have the shits for a week.

What happens if a Mexican doesn't pay his garbage bill?

They stop delivering.

♦

What do you call a picnic in Mexico?

A spicnic.

♦

Why are there no swimming pools in Mexico?

Because all the Mexicans who can swim have already crossed the border.

Racial Mixtures

What do Ethiopians say before picking their noses?

Grace.

♦

Why did the Ethiopians put in an urgent call to Dr. Scholls?

Because they are so hungry they're looking for jobs as odor eaters.

♦

What did the American Indian say when he put down the prime minister of Israel?

Me-Knockem-Begin.

♦

What's the difference between a Bhopalese citizen and a parking meter?

If Union Carbide destroyed 25,000 parking meters they'd be in trouble.

◆

What do they call feminine genital hygiene in India?

Bangladouche.

◆

What do you call a Hindu's penis?

Delhi meat.

◆

What is a Chinese-American prostitute's favorite holiday?

Erection Day.

◆

What's Chinese deli food?

Mao-Tse Tongue.

◆

Three Chinese women are talking about their husbands' tattoos.
   The first woman says, "My husband has a beautiful dragon on his arm."

The second woman says, "Well, my husband has a dragon on his chest."

Then the third woman speaks up. "That's nothing, my husband's draggin' on the ground."

◆

What do you call rat droppings in China?

Mao-Tse Dung.

◆

Did you hear about the biblical Japanese science fiction movie?

It's called *David and Godzilla*.

◆

What do they call a venereal disease in Germany?

Herr-pes.

◆

What's a slang expression for vagina in Germany?

Herr-Pie.

What do you call a prostitute from Toronto?

A Canadian Mount-ee.

◆

What do you call a British policeman with a foot fetish?

A Bobby Soxer.

◆

A Scotsman walked into a drugstore with a used condom in his hand. Holding it up to the pharmacist, he asked, "Can you retread this?"

"Of course not; just buy another rubber," the pharmacist replied.

"I'll think about it," said the Scotsman, and he walked out.

The next day, the Scotsman came back and said, "I've discussed it with the rest of the boys, and . . ."

◆

What's the difference between a Scotsman and a coconut?

You can always get a drink out of a coconut.

◆

If you put a fifty dollar bill on a hook and cast it off the roof, who would you catch:

A) Peter Pan
B) The Tooth Fairy
C) An Italian
D) A quick-thinking Irishman

An Italian, because there is no such thing as Peter Pan, the Tooth Fairy, or a quick-thinking Irishman.

◆

A Pole came to a German for advice. "I don't know what to do," said the Pole. "I've been married six weeks and still haven't managed to consummate my marriage."

The German had a chuckle and then proceeded to tell the Pole how to make love to a woman.

A week later, the Pole came back. "Well, I finally got the courage to do it last night," said the Pole sheepishly.

"And was it as great as I said it would be?" asked the German.

"Not really," said the Pole. "It just wasn't as pleasant as I imagined; it felt sort of funny to me."

"Never mind you; did she enjoy it?"

"Oh, well, yes, I believe very much so. She kept moaning and crying out."

"Yes, yes, go on," encouraged the German.

"And her toes curled up with each stroke!" exclaimed the Pole with macho pride.

Stunned, the German cried, "You idiot! You forgot to take off her panty hose!"

◆

What's a "pièce de résistance"?

A French virgin.

BUMPER STICKERS

Surfer: If it swells, ride it.

Proctologist: Eat shit. One million E. coli can't be wrong.

Prince Rainier: I still do it with grace.

Jack Horner: I do it with aplomb.

Gay relative of Gertrude Stein: A hose is a hose is a hose.